About the Book

UFOs . . extraterrestrial beings . . . do they exist? Have they visited our planet or tried to contact us? Will we ever communicate with them? In a thought-provoking discussion, noted science writer Melvin Berger explores the ways in which scientists have searched the universe for signs of intelligent life in space. Berger provides fascinating accounts of UFO sightings and encounters with mysterious beings—and suggests a plausible scientific explanation for all but a few of these bizarre incidents.

UFOs, ETs & VISITORS FROM SPACE

MELVIN BERGER

G.P. PUTNAM'S SONS
NEW YORK

Photo Credits
Cover photograph of a strange light descending to the ground was taken in Germany
on September 24, 1980, by Ann Dunetz, photographer.
Drawings on pages 11 and 12 are by Bud Handelsman.
Center for UFO Studies, pages 36, 37
Cornell University, page 50
Egyptian Tourist Authority, pages 70, 71 (top)
Hale Observatories, pages 40, 74
Mexican Tourist Office, page 64
Jukka Mikkola, page 25
NASA, pages 24, 31, 32, 47
National Archives, pages 17, 19, 21, 22, 28
National Radio Astronomy Observatory, page 44
New York Public Library Picture File, pages 57, 58, 62, 69
Peruvian Tourist Board, page 68
Scientific American, page 52
Every reasonable precaution has been taken to trace the owners of copyrighted material
and to make due acknowledgment. Any omission will be gladly rectified in future editions.

Library of Congress Cataloging-in-Publication Data
Berger, Melvin.   UFOs, ETs & visitors from space / Melvin Berger.
p.   cm.   Includes index.
Summary: Discusses the possibility of life on other planets, describes some of the best
known sightings of unidentified flying objects in recent times,
and speculates about possible visits to Earth made by extraterrestrials.
ISBN 0-399-61218-1
1. Unidentified flying objects—Juvenile literature. [1. Life on other planets.
2. Extraterrestrial beings.   3. Unidentified flying objects.] I. Title.
TL789.B478   1988   87-29094
001.9'42—dc19   CIP   AC

CONTENTS

UFOs are landing! This 16th-century print shows that the belief in UFOs was as strong in the past as it is today.

INTRODUCTION

The radio announcer on the evening news program of October 31, 1938, kept telling his listeners to remain calm. He assured them that the authorities were on the scene. They were taking all steps necessary to prevent a catastrophe.

Although he tried to sound calm, there was a note of panic in his voice. His fright was not hard to understand. He was reporting that a spaceship from Mars had just landed in New Jersey. In vivid details he described how the Martians were spreading throughout the countryside, capturing or killing any humans who tried to stop them.

Terror spread like wildfire among those in New Jersey and nearby states who were tuned in to the program. As people learned what was happening, they bolted their doors and locked their windows. Others hid beneath beds or crawled into cellars. Nearly everyone wanted to escape the alien invaders. While thousands threw their most valuable belongings into bags and fled their homes by foot or car, many others, too frightened to move, stayed glued to their radio sets.

But very soon the facts came out. The newscast about the landing of Martians on Earth was nothing more than fiction—a realistic dramatization of H. G. Wells's book *War of the Worlds.* What was very real—and totally unexpected—was the reaction of the public. Almost everyone was fully prepared to believe in an invasion from Mars!

The Belief in Life Elsewhere

In our own day, with men on the moon and spaceships on Mars, the belief in life elsewhere is perhaps greater than ever. But what facts do we actually have about intelligent beings in space? Do they exist? If so, what are they like? And what are our chances of communicating or visiting with them?

For the longest time, writers of science fiction and fantasy were the only ones seeking answers to these questions. But more recently, scientists have begun researching the possibility of life on planets that revolve around other suns. Using the tools and methods of modern science, highly trained researchers are shedding new light on an old subject—one that has long been hidden behind a screen of rumors, half-truths and unreliable observations.

Few deny the importance of exploring the possibility of intelligent life in space. Knowledge of life elsewhere will affect the ideas and beliefs we have about ourselves and our place in the universe. The thought that alien creatures may seek to destroy or conquer us is frightening—but not very likely. It is far more probable that beings from outer space, should they exist, are much more advanced than we are. Should they reach or contact our planet, they will have much to teach us.

In troubled times, people seem particularly eager to believe that there are better worlds outside our own. In part, this belief springs from the hope that humanity can, some day, achieve a more perfect society here on Earth. In addition, the search for other worlds in space satisfies our basic human curiosity about the unknown and expands the range of our understanding.

The Search for Extraterrestrial Beings

The search for other beings in the universe follows three basic paths. The first investigates sightings of UFOs—Unidentified Flying Objects. Here the aim is twofold: to determine if there are reliable sightings, seen by more than one observer, and to see if any of these encounters offer proof of contact with objects or beings from another planet.

The second tries to make contact with ETs, or extraterrestrials—creatures who live elsewhere in the universe. This consists mostly of listening for patterns of radio waves beamed from distant inhabited planets. But it also involves attempts to send our own messages into outer space.

Finally, there is an ongoing search for evidence that ETs have landed on Earth. These efforts involve finding some proof that there actually were visitors from space—physical signs of the landing or eyewitness accounts.

We are entering a wondrous new period in our understanding of worlds beyond our own. All the mystery and excitement that have attracted interest in the subject in the past is still there. But now, there is the added interest in the latest discoveries of science and research. In time we may even succeed in answering one of the most tantalizing questions of all: "Are we alone in the universe?"

I

TWO FABLES FOR OUR TIME

One day, a newly hatched crow was looking at his feathers. "Are all crows black like me?" he asked his mother.

"Of course they are," his mother answered. "Every crow in our flock is black. All the crows in the fields and forests for miles around are black. Everyone knows that every crow is black."

When he was a little bigger, the young crow went flying off by himself. After a while he saw another bird. It looked like a crow. It said "Caw, caw" like a crow. But it wasn't black. It was white!

The young crow flew over to the other bird. "Are you a crow?" he asked.

"Yes, I am," the white bird answered.

"But you're white instead of black," said the young crow.

"I know," replied the white crow. "The other crows in my flock are black. My parents are black crows. So I'm a crow, too. But I'm white."

The young crow quickly flew back to his mother. "I just saw a white crow!" he shouted in great excitement.

"You made a mistake," she said very firmly. "It was probably a dove."

"I'm sure it was a crow," he insisted.

His mother grew angry. "I've seen hundreds and hundreds of crows. They're all black. Crows are black. And that's final!"

The young crow just smiled.

Moral: It takes just one exception to prove that there are exceptions.

• • •

Suzy Owl and Billy Owl were the two young children of the Owl family. One Christmas morning Suzy and Billy were opening their presents. "Here's a pretty skirt from Aunt Nancy!" Suzy cried.

"And here's a great book about monsters from Grandma Eleanor," Billy said.

They kept on unwrapping their presents and calling out the name of the person who had given them each gift. Then suddenly Suzy said, "Here's a doll. But I don't know who gave it to me."

A minute later Billy said, "And I don't know who gave me this baseball mitt."

The two children looked at each other. "It must be Santa Claus," Suzy decided.

"Of course!" Billy agreed. "After all, we know who gave us all the other presents. This proves there is a Santa Claus!"

Mom and Dad Owl started to laugh. "We bought you the doll and mitt," they confessed. "We didn't put cards in the boxes as a joke. But neither of us is Santa Claus!"

Moral: When something happens that seems hard to figure out, look first for a simple explanation.

These fables have two very different morals. They also illustrate two different ways of thinking about UFOs and ETs.

The first fable suggests that even one unexplained UFO sighting or ET contact is proof enough that such things exist. According to the second fable, though, even happenings that are surprising and unexpected may have simple explanations.

Over the years there have been thousands of reports of UFO sightings and ET contacts. Almost all the incidents have been explained in ordinary ways. Still, a few remain unaccounted for. That leaves it up to each of us to decide what to think. Do you believe that only one unexplained UFO or ET incident proves that UFOs and ETs exist? Or do you believe that even though a few incidents are hard to figure out, they offer no real proof of life in other worlds?

2

UFOs

UFOs: abbreviation of Unidentified Flying Objects. Objects seen in the air or on land but of unknown source or origin.

It was three o'clock on the afternoon of June 24, 1947. Kenneth Arnold, a 32-year-old salesman, was flying his private plane from Chehalis to Yakima, Washington, to call on a customer. Suddenly, off to his left, Ken saw a bright flash of light. He noticed nine strange-looking aircraft flying toward Mount Rainier.

"I could see their outline quite plainly against the snow as they approached the mountain," he later said. "They flew very close to the mountaintops, directly south to southeast, down the hog's back of the range, flying like geese in a diagonal line, as if they were linked together.

"They were approximately 20 or 25 miles away," Arnold also reported, "and I couldn't see a tail on them. I watched for about three minutes . . . a chain of saucerlike things at least 5 miles long, swerving in and out of the high mountain peaks. They were flat like a pie pan and so shiny they reflected the sun like a mirror."

The startled pilot estimated that each silvery craft was 45 to 50 feet long. They seemed to be flying at a height of about 9,500 feet. And he put their speed at 1,700 miles an hour—about three times swifter than any existing plane! "I never saw anything so fast," he said later.

As Arnold watched in amazement, the strange-looking aircraft dove, soared and scooted this way and that before disappearing out of sight. After locating the point on his map, he continued his flight to the Yakima airport.

Arnold's account of the mysterious sightings created an absolute sensation. Newspapers and magazines around the world rushed to print stories about what he had seen. Using the pilot's words, they reported that the unidentified craft looked "like a saucer would if you skipped it across the water." That name caught on, and soon everyone was talking about "flying saucers."

The news reached the ears of officials in the U.S. Air Force. Since it is their job to protect the United States from air attack, they decided to investigate. After all, the craft that Arnold saw might threaten the nation's security.

An expert in military intelligence questioned Arnold at great length. He reported: "It is the personal opinion of the interviewer that Mr. Arnold actually saw what he stated that he saw. It is difficult to believe that a man of Mr. Arnold's character and apparent integrity would state that he saw objects and write up a report to the extent that he did if he did not see them."

• • •

In the little town of Maysville, Kentucky, on January 7, 1948, a number of people noted a strange-looking object in the sky overhead. Someone called the State Police. Several officers rushed out to look, and they, too, noticed something moving across the sky that they could not recognize. The police called the Godman Air Force Base near Louisville, Kentucky for more information. The control tower could offer no explanation. But they agreed to help identify the flying object.

Meanwhile, other reports of the same craft began pouring in. People from many different locations described it in similar terms: It was round, between 250 and 300 feet in diameter, metallic in color and glowing brightly. Everyone also said that it was heading westward at great speed.

By now the top commanders at Godman were at the control tower. None of them could identify the object. But while they were trying to decide what to do next, a flight of four F–51 jets from the Air National Guard passed nearby on a routine training flight. Since these very fast planes were already in the air, the officers at Godman asked the lead pilot, Captain Thomas Mantell, to investigate.

Captain Mantell banked his plane south to look for the object. Very soon he radioed the control tower, "Object traveling at half my speed and directly ahead of me and above. I'm going to take a closer look. It appears metallic and tremendous in size. I'm going to 20,000 feet." Then silence.

At 3:20 P.M. the Godman control tower got word that Captain Mantell's plane had crashed. Based on first reports, some said that he had made contact with the mysterious object. Others suspected that the unidentified object had somehow caused his plane to go down.

• • •

Clarence C. Chiles and John B. Whitted, two Eastern Airlines pilots, were flying from Houston, Texas, to Atlanta, Georgia, on the night of July 24, 1948. At 2:45 A.M., when they were a few miles southwest of Montgomery, Alabama, Captain Chiles noticed a red glow in the sky. Thinking it was some sort of advanced military plane, he told his copilot to look at the "new Army jet."

For ten seconds, as the two pilots watched, the craft advanced toward them from above and to the right. They later described it to FAA authorities as a huge cigar-shaped object, about 1,000 feet long and 30 feet across, without wings. Across its smooth surface were two rows of lighted windows.

Chiles said, "You could see right through the windows and out the other side." The bottom of the craft glowed a dark blue, and red-orange flames shot out the rear section.

Horror-struck, Chiles and Whitted watched the object come to within 700 feet of their plane. To avoid a collision, Captain Chiles pulled the plane sharply to the left. But despite his desperate maneuver, it still looked as if a midair crash was inevitable. Then, at the last possible instant, the "thing" veered to the right, just missing the passenger plane. Still flying at about 600 miles per hour, the craft suddenly rose up and disappeared in the clouds.

The pilots reported their sighting to the Air Force. Officials added this message to two other reports they had just received about the same craft. Observers at Robbins Air Force Base in Macon, Georgia, had described a brilliant light that flashed across the sky from north to south at about the same time. And two Air Force pilots who were flying near the Virginia–North Carolina state line had also seen a strange object flying in the direction of Montgomery, Alabama!

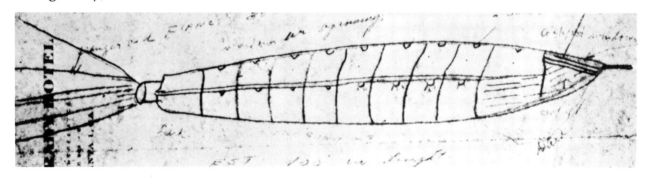

Right after the sighting, Whitted (top) and *Chiles (bottom)* made drawings of the UFO. Note how different they are.

On September 19, 1961, Betty and Barney Hill were driving on a deserted stretch of road through the White Mountains of New Hampshire. Just before three o'clock in the morning, both became aware of a light following them. Presently the light pulled ahead and a disk-shaped object, 65 feet across, stopped in front of the car.

Barney got out of the car to investigate. He saw alien creatures standing in the windows of the craft. One of the strange, humanlike beings was grinning broadly. Terrified by what he witnessed, Barney ran back to the car and sped away.

Much later, the Hills realized that there were about two hours on that night that they could not account for. Both of them became very anxious. Betty began suffering from frightening nightmares. Barney developed an ulcer.

In December of 1962, the Hills went to psychiatrist Dr. Benjamin Simon in Boston for treatment. Dr. Simon decided to hypnotize the couple as a way of relieving their mental stress. While under hypnosis, the Hills were helped to recall what happened during those "missing" two hours. What came out, separately, from each of their stories, proved to be amazingly similar and one of the most exciting—and baffling—of all UFO stories.

Both Betty and Barney told of being brought inside the "silver metal" craft by "short, grotesque" creatures who were about 5 feet tall, had "grayish" skin, very large "dark black" eyes, no ears and tiny noses. The creatures examined the two of them, but did neither any harm. The Hills were also shown the maps the aliens had used to find Earth from their home in the Zeta Reticuli star system. Just before the aliens departed, they released the Hills and warned them to forget all that had happened.

Dr. Simon's medical report included Betty's re-creation of the creatures' map. As soon as the report was made public, a number of researchers tried to plot the location on published star maps. Several possible matches were

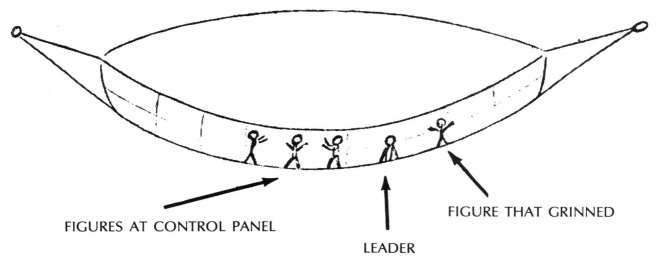

FIGURES AT CONTROL PANEL

LEADER

FIGURE THAT GRINNED

This is Barney Hill's sketch of the object and creatures he saw.

suggested, but experts could not agree on the home port of the mysterious spaceship.

• • •

On December 13, 1961, George E. Weber was walking across the parking lot of George Washington University in Washington, D.C., when a guard pointed out a strange-looking object in the sky. Meanwhile, William John Meyer, Jr., who was driving his car and waiting for a traffic light to change, also noted the same object overhead.

All three descriptions of the object were similar—dark gray in color, diamond-shaped, about 20 feet long and moving silently at a height of about 1,500 feet.

Weber mentioned a light shining from the bottom of the object. Meyer told of an orange-brown glow from the center area. The craft had neither wings nor propellers and left no vapor trail in the air. The two men in the parking lot had it in view for about three minutes. Meyer could watch only for a minute before the beeping horns of the cars he was blocking forced him to move along with the traffic.

• • •

Just before six o'clock on the evening of April 24, 1964, Sergeant Lonnie Zamora of the Socorro, New Mexico, Police Department spotted a speeding black Chevrolet. Zamora began chasing the car south near the city limits when, in the policeman's words, "I heard a roar and saw a flame in the sky to the southwest, some distance away, possibly a half-mile or a mile." He said the flame was "bluish and sort of orange, too." Giving up the chase, Zamora decided to investigate the mysterious object instead.

To reach the source of the noise and the flame, the officer pulled off the highway and drove along a rough gravel road. About 150 or 200 yards south of the road, Zamora saw an object that looked like an overturned car, but was all bright and shiny as though made of aluminum. There was no sign of the flames he had seen before.

Standing next to the craft were two figures in white coveralls. Zamora said they were "normal in shape, but possibly they were small adults or large kids." When one turned to look at the police car, the creature "seemed startled, seemed to quickly jump somewhat."

As Zamora steered his car toward the craft, the figures scampered back into the object. A burst of blue and orange flame shot out from under the craft and it emitted the same loud roar he had heard before. As it rose up into the air slowly, Zamora noticed that it had no visible doors or windows, only some red markings on the side.

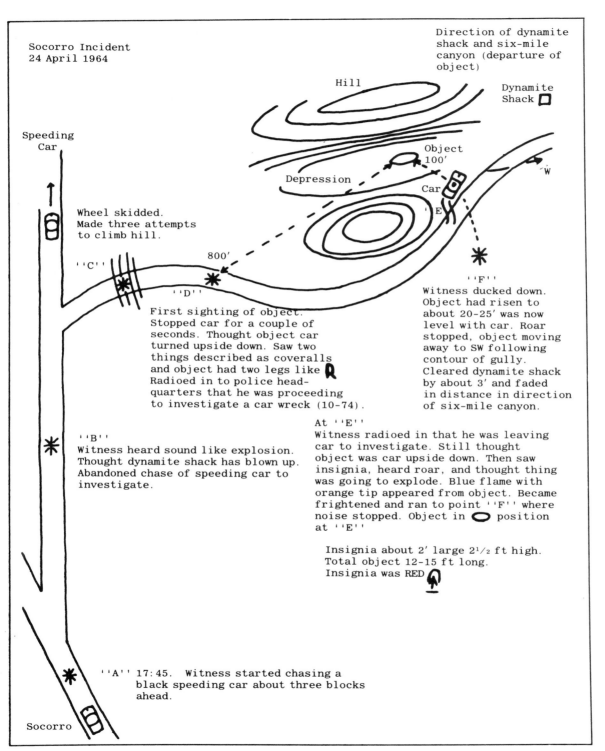

Socorro Incident
24 April 1964

Direction of dynamite shack and six-mile canyon (departure of object)

Hill

Dynamite Shack

Speeding Car

Object 100'

Car

Depression

W

Wheel skidded. Made three attempts to climb hill.

800'

E

''C''

''D''

''F''
Witness ducked down. Object had risen to about 20-25' was now level with car. Roar stopped, object moving away to SW following contour of gully. Cleared dynamite shack by about 3' and faded in distance in direction of six-mile canyon.

First sighting of object. Stopped car for a couple of seconds. Thought object car turned upside down. Saw two things described as coveralls and object had two legs like Radioed in to police headquarters that he was proceeding to investigate a car wreck (10-74).

At ''E''
Witness radioed in that he was leaving car to investigate. Still thought object was car upside down. Then saw insignia, heard roar, and thought thing was going to explode. Blue flame with orange tip appeared from object. Became frightened and ran to point ''F'' where noise stopped. Object in ⬭ position at ''E''

''B''
Witness heard sound like explosion. Thought dynamite shack has blown up. Abandoned chase of speeding car to investigate.

Insignia about 2' large 2½ ft high.
Total object 12-15 ft long.
Insignia was RED

''A'' 17:45. Witness started chasing a black speeding car about three blocks ahead.

Socorro

Lonnie Zamora prepared this map and description of the sighting at Socorro.

Terrified by the noise and flame, the officer turned and started to pull away. The object's roar rose to a high-pitched whine and then stopped altogether. When Zamora looked back, he saw the object skimming away about 15 feet above the ground.

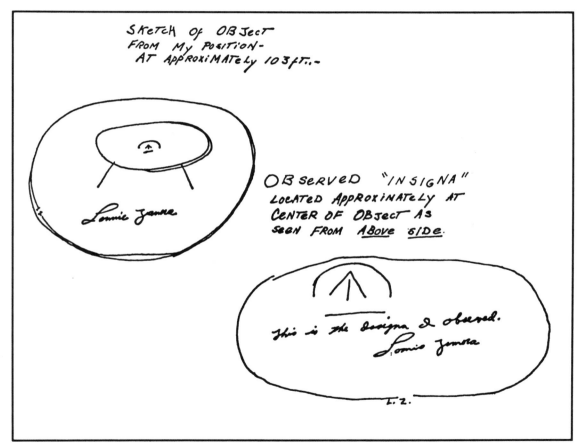

Zamora drew the object and the red markings that he saw.

Zamora radioed in an account of his experience and Sergeant Sam Chavez of the New Mexico State Police appeared on the scene. The two men took note of the scorched ground and burned bushes where Zamora had encountered the craft. They also found four shallow holes in the ground—about 12 inches long and 1 inch deep—arranged in a diamond pattern. The bushes had been burnt, they assumed, by the flames, and they also assumed the four holes had been created by the landing feet of the craft.

• • •

Launched on July 16th, 1969, the Apollo 11 space shot had three astronauts on board—Neil Armstrong, Edwin Aldrin and Michael Collins. The historic flight was the first to place a human being on the moon.

After their return, certain stories began circulating about bizarre happenings on their trip. On the second day, when they were about halfway to the moon, it was said, the crew observed some shiny white objects flying alongside their ship and keeping pace with them. They supposedly photographed the objects. Two days later, they again saw the objects and again recorded the sighting on film.

According to some reports, the astronauts noted two objects flying together in close formation. At times they would come close together. Then they would separate. Both appeared to be emitting some sort of liquid. After watching their movements in space, the astronauts decided the objects were under intelligent control.

The report of astronaut sightings of unidentified objects was taken very seriously. Because astronauts are highly trained as pilots and scientists, they are considered very reliable observers. In this case, not only had they presumably sighted the objects, but they had also taken photos of them. It had long been expected that if there are intelligent beings elsewhere in the universe, they would be very interested in our space shots.

The Apollo XI space mission is famous because it placed the first men—Neil Armstrong and Edwin Aldrin—on the moon.

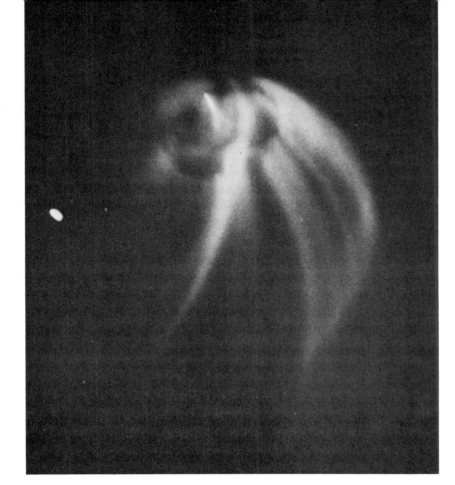

Early on the morning of September 20, 1977, people in Russia and Finland saw a glowing jellyfish in the dark sky.

• • •

It was just about 4:00 A.M. in the pre-dawn hours of September 20, 1977. In Leningrad, Helsinki and many places in between, residents who were awake at that hour observed something absolutely terrifying. One eyewitness said that it looked like a glowing "jellyfish" hovering over the Russian city of Petrozavodsk. Shaped like a huge star, it glowed brightly in the almost pitch-dark sky. And pouring out and down from this disk were fine rays of light, which some said looked like a shower of shiny raindrops.

After a while the rays disappeared. The object changed its shape, becoming more like a semicircle. And it began heading off in the direction of Lake Onega. The half-circle shone with a bright light—red in the middle and white at the sides. Observers reported that they could see it for as long as 12 minutes.

The rumors and stories that followed this sighting were quite amazing. People reported that the hanging arms of the so-called jellyfish had dug holes in the sidewalks of the various cities over which it had passed. Some home owners complained that those same rays had drilled holes in the glass of their windows. A number of Russian dockworkers took it as a signal of the beginning of an American invasion of Russia. One doctor grumbled that the object passing overhead made his ambulance go out of control. Large groups of people said they smelled ozone in the air for days after the sighting.

• • •

Colonel Osires Silva is a trained aeronautical engineer as well as the head of Brazil's state-owned oil company. Because of his background and position everyone listened very carefully to what he had to say when his private plane landed at the airport at São José dos Campos on May 19, 1986.

Silva told how he and his pilot had seen a strange light in the air. He described "a dancing point in the sky." The two observers estimated the object's speed at about 900 miles per hour.

On checking with the control tower, it was learned that some unidentified objects were also being picked up on the radar screen. The airport authorities quickly called the Brazilian Defense Center. They sent up six of their fastest jets to locate and identify these mysterious lights.

Although all the pilots saw the lights, the planes they were flying could not catch up with the objects emitting them. After some three hours the pilots lost sight of the lights entirely. They also disappeared from the radar screen.

Even though the Brazilian Air Force investigated the incident, they never released their findings.

These have been among the best-known sightings of UFOs in recent years. At first, the accounts were generally accepted to be true. Like the black crow finding the white crow in our first fable, many people believed it takes just one UFO sighting to prove that UFOs exist.

Later, however, a number of investigators tried to discover whether or not these reports were accurate. Like Suzy and Billy Owl in the second fable, they wanted to see if there were simple explanations of events that were hard to understand. Very often what they found was completely different from the original reports.

The Kenneth Arnold Case

This case proved to be one of the simplest to understand. Bright sunlight shining on clouds among mountain peaks frequently creates optical illusions, making things seem real that are not. One effect that has been noted often is the optical illusion of disks of light that seem to be floating in the air. There is every reason to believe that such round, flat, thin objects are what Arnold saw. The nine disks were merely a false impression of "flying saucers" caused by the particular relationship of the sun, clouds and mountains at the time.

The Captain Mantell Case

Investigators of the Mantell incident found that the captain had been chasing a Skyhook balloon. The incident occurred, however, at a time when the Skyhook balloon was still a military secret. No one outside the program knew that it even existed.

The balloon, it was discovered, had a metallic surface, measured 100 feet across and carried various scientific measuring instruments. Captain Mantell did not crash because of any encounter with a UFO. The Air Force authorities said that he flew too high without oxygen and blacked out.

The Eastern Airlines Case

For nearly twenty years, the report by the two Eastern Airlines pilots puzzled experts. Then, on March 3, 1968, three observers in Tennessee, six in Indiana and three in Ohio reported a UFO that looked exactly like the one Chiles and Whitted had seen. It even included the row of windows lit from within!

When experts from the Air Force started working on this case, they discovered that the Russians had put a spacecraft into orbit on March 2, 1968. The day of the "sighting," one of the rocket boosters fell back down toward earth and burned up in the atmosphere. What appeared to be a spaceship was the booster shell. And what seemed to be a row of lit windows was the red-hot fragments breaking off the burning shell. Since the Chiles-Whitted UFO looked the same, it was probably the falling booster from a secret space shot.

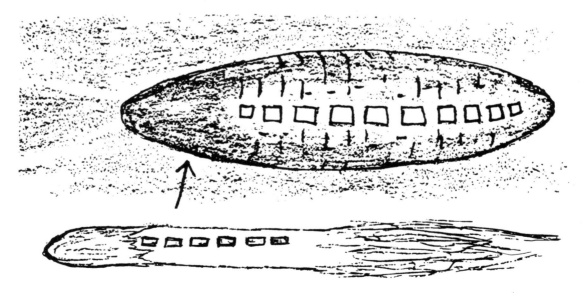

In 1968, people in Tennessee (top) and Indiana (bottom) drew sketches that looked remarkably like the Chiles and Whitted sketches. But it was known that the '68 sightings were of the falling booster rocket from a Russian space shot!

The Hill Case

The 1961 encounter of Betty and Barney Hill with "alien creatures" was very convincing. How else could one explain their identical stories of abduction by creatures from the spaceship? In fact, this case was so persuasive that it became the basis for a book, *Interrupted Journey* (1966), by John Fuller, and a TV movie, *The UFO Incident,* aired on NBC in 1975.

However, a breakthrough came in 1975. Dr. Simon, the psychiatrist who spent hundreds of hours treating the Hills, broke his silence. At long last, he gave his professional opinion of the case.

The doctor pointed out that Betty had been an avid reader of science fiction magazines. Her sister was also very interested in tales of interplanetary travel and adventure. Often the two women would discuss some of the more terrifying UFO stories together. So it seemed obvious, Dr. Simon concluded, that Betty's nightmares originated in these fictional stories.

As the doctor also learned, Betty retold many of these stories to her husband. Since they had the same frightening UFO tales in the back of their minds, it was not surprising that they both imagined the same encounter with the UFO and its creatures.

Robert Sheaffer, a UFO investigator, took another tack in researching the Hill case. He studied the weather records and the positions of stars and planets on the night of the event. What the Hills saw, he believes, was the planet Jupiter bursting forth from behind some clouds. This sight, combined with the fact that it was late and they were tired, convinced the couple that something was chasing them. According to other experts, this strange illusion has been reported a number of times before.

The Weber–Meyer Sightings

The 1961 Weber–Meyer sighting in Washington, D.C., is still listed as an unsolved case. After nearly thirty years, no one has been able to confirm it either as a known object, a natural event or a true encounter with a UFO.

The Zamora Case

The Lonnie Zamora sighting in the New Mexico desert is, according to UFO expert Major Hector Quintanilla of the U.S. Air Force, "the best-documented case in the Air Force files." Dr. J. Allen Hynek (1911-1986), an astronomer, consultant on UFOs to the Air Force, founder of the Center for UFO Studies and the leading UFO researcher, has said that "a real physical event occurred on the outskirts of Socorro that afternoon."

Philip Klass, an electrical engineer, and also a student of UFOs, has come up with one possible explanation. Klass thinks that Zamora may have seen an unusual form of lightning. This type appears as a bright, shiny ball, not as the usual streak of light across the sky. A lightning ball can be several feet across and so appear to be a solid object. And it may be seen at any height—from just above the ground to high in the air.

Klass also says that Zamora's description of the "bluish and sort of orange" flame also fits the color of a ball of lightning. As for the two figures in white that Zamora noticed, Klass says they could have been wisps of electrified gas coming from the lightning. To the frightened police officer, however, they looked like small men.

The Apollo 11 Incident

The Apollo 11 incident proved to be an out-and-out fake. When Neil Armstrong was asked about seeing UFOs, he answered, "We didn't see them, and with what we . . . are doing in space, that's a real wonder." NASA official Charles Redmond adds, "We don't have any UFO secrets."

One photograph of Earth taken from Apollo 11 did, however, show a bright white object floating in the air. But upon further investigation, it proved to be nothing more than a piece of metal that had broken off when the lunar module was released. In the same way, movie film shot from inside the spacecraft reveals a number of strange lights and shapes. All the experts agree, however, that they are simply reflections and glares in the window.

A photo taken from Apollo XI did show a white object in space. But it was nothing more than a piece of metal that had broken off from the spacecraft!

The strange lights and shapes (top) were just re-flections in the window. Some photos were re-touched (bottom) to make them look like UFOs.

It now seems clear that the early reports of UFOs involving Apollo 11 were based on false quotes and transcripts of conversations between the crew and Mission Control. Also, it was discovered that someone had retouched the photos to make them look as though UFOs were present. Nevertheless, the desire to believe in UFOs is very strong in some people. Even when NASA released the original transcripts and the original photos, which did not show UFOs, some Americans continued to think that the Apollo 11 crew had seen UFOs. A few even charged that NASA was hiding the truth!

The "Jellyfish" UFO

A study of the records shows that at 3:58 on the morning of the "jellyfish" sightings, Russia launched an artificial satellite from a secret base near Plesetsk. Since this was a covert operation, there was no public mention of the launch. Previous launchings from the same site had never been seen due to the fact that a pre-dawn mist usually covers the area.

The morning was very clear, however, when the glowing mass with flowing tentacles appeared near Plesetsk. The unusual weather made the rocket quite visible in the dark sky. And the booster's five separate sets of jets sent out vapor trails that could be seen clearly—and closely resembled the trailing feelers of a jellyfish!

The Colonel Silva Sighting

The results of the Brazilian Air Force investigation of the "dancing point" of light that Colonel Silva watched have never been made public. Nor have any other scientists been able to explain what the colonel, his pilot and the six pilots of the Air Force jets observed or what the radar screen showed that night.

James Oberg, a leading UFO researcher, points out that radar can be fooled by birds, insects or certain weather conditions. But neither he nor any of the others who have looked into the case has succeeded in identifying the mysterious lights. Colonel Silva's sighting, therefore, remains another significant case of an unsolved UFO encounter.

UFOs in Perspective

Sightings of UFOs are nothing new. As long ago as A.D. 98, a number of ancient Romans reported seeing a round burning shield flashing across the sky. Another sighting from around that time was of a giant globe, brighter than the sun, coming down to Earth and then flying off again. In fact, all through the Middle Ages people related tales about strange objects and unexplained lights that they saw in the sky—and sometimes on land as well.

What *is* new are the efforts of scientists to study UFOs. Soon after Kenneth Arnold reported seeing flying saucers in 1947, the U.S. Air Force set up an office to investigate all such sightings to make sure they were not part of a military attack or invasion. The inquiry was later given the name Project Blue Book. In 1969 the project was brought to a close when the Air Force concluded that UFOs did not threaten the nation's security.

Besides the Air Force, many private organizations set up UFO investigations. Some of them are still in operation. Worldwide, reports on UFO sightings still pour in at the rate of about 100 a day!

To help in the study of UFOs, scientist J. Allen Hynek divided UFO sightings into six types.

The first three are distant observations:

1. Bright lights seen in the night sky.
2. Bright ovals or disks seen in the daytime sky.
3. Objects detected only by radar.

The final three are much closer and thus more exciting:

4. Close encounters of the first kind—sighting an unidentified object on Earth.

5. Close encounters of the second kind—sighting an unidentified object on Earth and tracing its physical effects on things or beings.

This old woodcut shows a sighting of UFOs in Germany on April 24, 1561.

6. Close encounters of the third kind—sighting an unidentified object on Earth and making physical contact with the object or its occupants.

Most UFO reports fall into one of the first three of Dr. Hynek's categories. But experts find eventually that most of them, perhaps 90 percent or more, are not true UFOs. They are really IFOs—Identified Flying Objects.

According to these experts, people may be fooled into thinking they are making a Type One sighting when they catch an unusual or unexpected view of a plane, a meteor, the very bright planet Venus or one of the other planets. Weather balloons, particular cloud formations, artificial satellites and blimps account for a large percentage of Type Two observations. False radar signals can come either from flocks of birds, swarms of insects or unexplained radar waves, called "angels."

When Project Blue Book stopped operating, it had studied over 12,000 UFO sightings. Of the total number, the experts were able to explain well over 90 percent of the reported incidents. In over 2,000 of the cases, the observers were found to be seeing Venus or another planet, a particularly bright star or some other natural astronomical body or event. In another 1,500 cases, the object sighted proved to be an airplane. Nearly 800 more were glimpses of artificial satellites, and about 500 were balloons. A total of about 6,500 were false reports, posed or retouched photos, strange cloud formations, birds, insects and just plain human error.

When all was said and done, however, there remained about 700 events for which no explanation could be found, either natural or man-made. What do the experts say about these?

Major Hector Quintanilla, former director of Project Blue Book, insists that there are no UFOs. He cites the absence of even one fully confirmed report of a UFO sighting. Astronomer Carl Sagan concurs. A true sighting, he expects, would have many reliable witnesses all coming forward at the same time.

Some people think these 1974 photos show a UFO coming to Earth. Others believe they are a fake.

Other experts make these points: UFOs could not land and then take off without leaving significant evidence of the tremendous force needed to launch or slow down a spaceship. Since a spaceship would have to travel an immense distance to arrive on Earth, it would not just appear in a remote area, stay for a few minutes and then quickly fly away. Most likely it would stay for a period of time and make better contact with the Earth's inhabitants. And with all the military air defense and civilian air traffic systems now operating, it is virtually impossible for any aircraft to enter the Earth's air space without being detected.

Still, in a February 1987 Gallup poll, almost half of all Americans said they believe in UFOs. Some had had UFO experiences themselves and don't accept the scientists' explanations. Many more had read or seen very dramatic accounts of the most exciting of these encounters. For all these people, the unsolved, unexplained UFO events are enough to convince them that there are living beings that have come to Earth from the outer reaches of space in what we call UFOs.

3
ETs

ETs: abbreviation of extraterrestrials. Living creatures on other planets, usually limited to beings advanced enough to send or receive messages.

The belief that there are other forms of life in the universe stretches far back in history. About 2,000 years ago the Roman poet Lucretius wrote, "So we must realize that there are other worlds in other parts of the universe, with races of different men and different animals."

In modern times, as scientists have begun the serious search for life elsewhere, they have given such creatures a name. They call them ETs.

Despite thousands of years of speculation and more than thirty years of research, no one is yet sure whether alien beings exist in space. The scientists who believe there are ETs reason in this way:

Living beings are made up of a combination of organic compounds. They are able to reproduce and evolve, or change, from generation to generation. And from what we now know, such beings can arise only on a planet.

Through their telescopes on Earth, astronomers can see at least one trillion trillion stars (1,000,000,000,000,000,000,000,000). Assume that just

Among the trillions and trillions of stars we can see, astronomers believe there may be a trillion planets with ETs.

one out of every million stars has a planet orbiting around it. That makes one million trillion (1,000,000,000,000,000,000,000) planets. Then, if only one planet in a million has the proper conditions on which life depends, there would still be a trillion planets occupied by ETs.

A very famous experiment done in 1953 showed one way that life may have started on Earth some five billion years ago. At that early time the Earth's atmosphere is believed to have contained four gases—water vapor, hydrogen, methane and ammonia.

Researchers Stanley Miller (b. 1930) and Harold Urey (b. 1893) placed samples of the four gases into a container. They passed electric sparks through the mixture, much as lightning bolts flashed through the Earth's atmosphere ages ago. After a few days they found they had created some organic compounds and some amino acids—the building blocks of living tissue.

For living beings to develop from these beginnings, the conditions must be suitable. The planet must be the right distance from its sun, so that the temperature is not too hot or too cold. There must also be plenty of water and enough oxygen in the air to sustain life. And the atmosphere must be thick enough to keep out ultraviolet rays and other dangerous radiation from space.

Beings in Space

Given the right environment, what are the chances of life arising and developing on planets other than Earth?

With an estimated trillion planets where life could arise, many astronomers say that the odds are good that life exists somewhere else. Also, most scientists now hold that since life on Earth originated in more than one spot, it may also be likely that life arose at several places in the universe.

Supporters of this "life elsewhere" idea cite a discovery of biologist Melvin Calvin (b. 1911). Calvin found organic compounds in meteorites that landed on Earth. Since meteorites come from outer space, the presence of these compounds suggests that there is some form of life out there.

Living beings can be found under the most varied conditions on Earth—from the bottom of the deepest ocean to the top of the highest mountain, from the icy polar regions to steamy tropical jungles. If life can adapt to such extreme conditions on Earth, isn't it reasonable to expect that living beings can develop and grow on different planets?

Astronomer Fred Hoyle (b. 1915) asserts that it is not even necessary for life to start on several planets. He suggests that it could begin in just one place and spread from there to other planets in the universe.

Among the scientists who take the "no life elsewhere" tack is biologist George Gaylord Simpson (b. 1902). The origin of life on Earth, he says, was an extremely random happening. He finds it hard to imagine the same circumstances coming together more than once. Evolution on Earth, he concludes, is unique.

Simpson also says that the evolutionary process never occurs twice in exactly the same way. No known species ever appeared, disappeared and then reappeared. Dinosaurs developed and then became extinct. There were no dinosaurs before them, nor will any dinosaurs ever appear again.

Fred Hoyle and the others who believe in the theory of life elsewhere have a notion that ETs resemble humans. They cannot imagine a more efficient, practical form than the one that has evolved on Earth.

David Laup of the University of Chicago regards this as a narrow, self-centered view. There is no evidence one way or another about the appearance of ETs, so he feels it is limiting to argue about the way they look.

These examples show that scientists hold different views on beings in space. But on one point everyone agrees: Any ETs that come into contact with us will be more advanced than we are. The reason is that we have just learned how to send signals and rockets into outer space. We are like newborn babies. It is therefore almost a certainty that any ETs that come to Earth will be operating on a higher, rather than lower, level than we are. That is why the search for ETs is usually called SETI, Search for Extraterrestrial Intelligence.

SETIs

Before the first modern SETI, a number of leading scientists proposed ways to make contact with beings beyond planet Earth. The great German mathematician and astronomer Karl Gauss (1777-1855) wanted humans to plant enormous fields with long lines of trees. His idea was to arrange the trees in a way that would show observers on a distant planet proof of the Pythagorean theorem. The Bohemian astronomer Joseph von Littrow (1781-1840) thought of digging huge ditches in the Sahara desert in various geometric forms. By filling the ditches with kerosene and setting them on fire, we would have created patterns visible from very far away. Physicist Nikola Tesla (1856-1943) actually sent radio signals out into space and was convinced that they were being received by ETs somewhere beyond Earth.

The era of truly scientific SETI really began in 1959 under the direction of the well-known astronomer Dr. Frank Drake (b. 1930). He called his research Project Ozma, after the Princess in the fictional land of Oz. According to Dr. Drake, Oz was "a place very far away, difficult to reach, and populated by exotic beings"—a good description of the imagined home of ETs.

Project Ozma used a radio telescope—one of the most amazing instruments of modern science—as its main tool. The radio telescope is a huge antenna, shaped like a metal dish, and up to 1,000 feet in diameter. It was originally designed to receive the natural radio signals given off by the atoms in stars, clouds of interstellar gas and various other bodies in space.

For Project Ozma, Dr. Drake also listened to the radio waves from space. He expected that most would be from natural sources. But among them might be some special ones—signals with a form or pattern different from natural radio waves. These radio waves might come from an artificial source, perhaps intelligent beings in space.

Dr. Drake focused the radio telescope at the National Radio Astronomy Observatory (NRAO) at Green Bank, West Virginia, on two nearby stars, Tau Ceti and Epsilon Eridani. These stars closely resemble our sun. For that reason they are thought more likely to be circled by planets on which life

The radio telescope is the main tool in the search for ETs.

might have developed. Tau Ceti is located at a distance of 11.9 light-years away; Epsilon Eridani is 10.7 light-years away. (A light-year is the distance light, traveling at 186,000 miles per second, covers in a year; it is about 6 trillion miles.)

The Project Ozma team at Green Bank began listening for nonnatural radio signals. From Tau Ceti they could detect nothing. But when they pointed the telescope at Epsilon Eridani, they got a signal they could not recognize!

Since radio telescopes sometimes pick up radio signals from sources on Earth, Dr. Drake's first step was to look for man-made sources. He could find none.

Once again Dr. Drake aimed the radio telescope at Epsilon Eridani. This time he heard the star's usual radio signal. But the special radio waves were no longer audible! Had ETs been transmitting and stopped? Or was there some other explanation?

After significant study, Dr. Drake reached a simple conclusion. The unusual signals probably stemmed from a secret military operation involving advanced electronic equipment. But since the information was not available to him, he could not be certain.

During 1959 and 1960 Dr. Drake and his coworkers spent 150 hours listening to radio signals from the two stars. Except for the one unexplained signal, they did not hear anything that might be considered a message from an ET.

Yet Project Ozma was very important. It set the model for most of the SETI projects that followed. To date there have been about forty officially recognized SETI efforts, some of them still continuing. In addition, many amateurs listen for radio waves on their own equipment. And radio astronomers, as they go about their regular research, also look out for signals that might indicate intelligent beings.

"Tuning" the Radio Telescopes

Radio waves, whether from the sky or from Earth broadcasting stations, vary in frequency. Radio stations broadcast at different frequencies so that their signals can be heard distinctly. Home radios, therefore, must be tuned to different frequencies to pick up various stations' programs.

But how could Drake and the other astronomers know at what frequency to tune their radio telescope to detect signals from ETs?

In 1959, Philip Morrison and Giuseppe Cocconi suggested setting the radio telescope at a frequency of 1,420 MHz. The unit of frequency is the hertz, which is abbreviated Hz. One Hz is one cycle per second. Since radio waves are measured in millions of cycles per second, frequencies are usually given as megahertz, MHz, meaning millions of cycles per second. Thus 1,420 MHz is 1,420 million cycles per second.

Morrison and Cocconi chose this frequency for a particular reason. Hydrogen is the most abundant element in the universe; it makes up an estimated 65 percent of all matter. The electrons in hydrogen atoms change the way they spin from time to time. And each time the electron flips its orbit, the individual hydrogen atoms send out a tiny pulse of radio energy—at 1,420 MHz! (Radio waves can also be measured by length, instead of frequency. The hydrogen radio waves are about 21 cm, or 8.4 inches, long.)

Any civilization advanced enough to send messages, they reasoned, would know about hydrogen and its frequency. It seemed the most logical frequency for trying to communicate with others in the universe.

Other SETI

In 1967 Jocelyn Bell, a graduate student at Cambridge University in England, was doing research on the university's newly installed radio telescope. In one point of the sky she was amazed to find a radio signal that flashed on and off in short, regular bursts, or pulses. Each pulse lasted just over one second. No star or any event known to astronomers had ever produced such a signal.

Jocelyn Bell and other astronomers had a thought that the on/off radio signals might be a very simple message from ETs in space. Half-joking, Bell named the source of the signals LGM-1—Little Green Men, No. 1.

As it turned out, Bell was not picking up ETs at all. For the first time in history, she had succeeded in detecting radio signals from a certain kind of star, a pulsar. Pulsars are huge stars that have exploded and then collapsed into a tightly packed core. The core spins rapidly, sending a very powerful radio beam out in one direction. The repeated, short flashes Bell received were the signals emitted each time the spinning radio beam was aimed at Earth!

The search for a sign of intelligent life in the universe also continued at Green Bank. Several astronomers there turned their radio telescopes on a group of twelve stars that they suspected might be home to ETs. In 1977 they were quite sure that they had found something.

At around 8:00 A.M. every morning, when their telescopes faced the same part of the sky, they picked up a particular set of signals. They could not recognize the pattern. But one thing they knew: The strong, clear radio waves were not coming from a natural source.

As with Project Ozma, they first had to decide if the signals were coming from a source on Earth. A simple explanation soon came to light. Many of the workers at the NRAO changed shift at eight o'clock. A number of the arriving and leaving staff members had CB radios in their cars. The very sensitive radio telescope was picking up their messages!

On a hill 30 miles west of Boston sits a radio telescope that is 84 feet in diameter. Under the direction of Paul Horowitz, a professor of physics at Harvard University, it is being used in the most advanced, thorough SETI ever attempted. The radio telescope is collecting radio waves from the skies 24 hours a day, 365 days a year.

This radio telescope is connected to a powerful computer that Professor Horowitz built by hooking together 144 separate computers. The computer, which can handle up to 75 million bits of information a minute, continuously monitors the radio waves collected by the telescope. Once a day Professor

Horowitz, or a member of his staff, checks the computer printout for signs of artificial, rather than natural, radio signals.

The combined radio telescope-computer that Professor Horowitz is using has fantastic abilities. Instead of listening at only one frequency, 1,420 MHz, it stays tuned to 8.4 million different frequencies—all at the same time! This arrangement is called META for Megachannel Extraterrestrial Array. As Horowitz says, META "accomplishes more searching in one minute than could have been done in 100,000 years with the first receiver [the radio telescope used in Project Ozma]."

META has been in operation since 1983, yet Dr. Horowitz still has not found any trace of signals beamed to Earth from an alien civilization. But he is not discouraged. Some day he fully expects to receive a message from afar, since he believes there are beings in space capable of communicating with us. "There's nothing extraordinary about our sun and nothing special about our Earth," says Horowitz. "Take anything in astronomy. There's never just one. Usually if you can find one of something, like some strange star, then people find handfuls, dozens, hundreds of these things."

Receiving radio waves surely has exciting possibilities. But they are only one way of communicating. What about other ways of trying to learn about ETs?

"Hello out there!"

In 1972 one of the boldest attempts to contact an alien civilization was made. American scientists sent a "letter" to any ETs that might be there to receive it. Scientists launched Pioneer 10 from the Kennedy Space Center in March of that year. They "addressed" the letter not to a destination within the solar system, but to a point in space between the constellations Taurus and Orion. But, even traveling at the incredible speed of 21,600 miles per *second*, it will take Pioneer 10 over 100,000 years to come near the stars in that area!

Pioneer 10 is carrying a gold-plated aluminum plaque, 6 by 10 inches. Inscribed on it are drawings of a nude man and woman, the Pioneer spacecraft, the solar system, Pioneer's path through the planets, the location of the sun in relation to the galaxy and a diagram of the hydrogen atom. Perhaps some ET will spot Pioneer 10 during its long journey, will understand at least some of the drawings and will figure out a way to contact us. On June 13, 1983, Pioneer became the first man-made object to reach the outer bounds of our solar system. Hundreds or thousands of years from now it may succeed in finally delivering its message.

Pioneer 10 carries a metal plate with several messages for ETs.

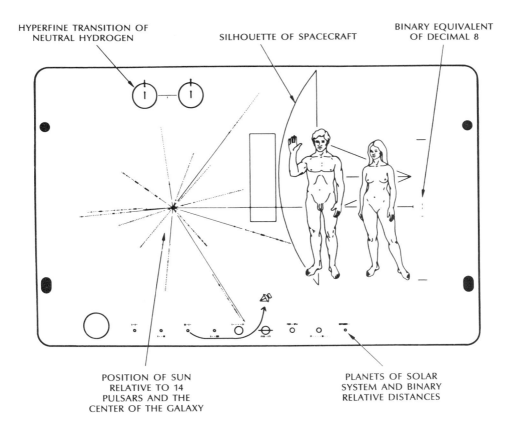

HYPERFINE TRANSITION OF
NEUTRAL HYDROGEN

SILHOUETTE OF SPACECRAFT

BINARY EQUIVALENT
OF DECIMAL 8

POSITION OF SUN
RELATIVE TO 14
PULSARS AND THE
CENTER OF THE GALAXY

PLANETS OF SOLAR
SYSTEM AND BINARY
RELATIVE DISTANCES

At 1:30 on the afternoon of November 16, 1974, Dr. Drake of Project Ozma tried sending rather than listening for radio messages from space. The message he beamed came from the world's largest nonmovable radio telescope at Arecibo, Puerto Rico. The waves were directed toward a group of about 300,000 stars in what astronomers called globular cluster M–13, which is about 25,000 light-years distant.

The radio telescope at Arecibo, Puerto Rico was used to send a radio mesage deep into space.

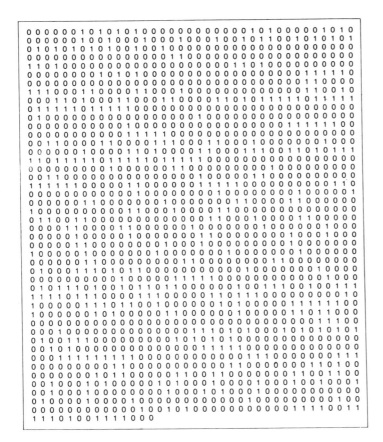

```
0 0 0 0 0 1 0 1 0 1 0 1 0 0 0 0 0 0 0 0 0 0 0 0 1 0 1 0 0 0 0 0 1 0 1 0
0 0 0 0 0 1 0 0 1 0 0 0 1 0 0 0 1 0 0 0 1 0 0 1 0 1 0 1 1 0 0 1 0 1 0 1 0 1
0 1 0 1 0 1 0 1 0 1 0 0 1 0 0 1 0 0 1 0 0 0 0 0 0 0 0 0 0 0 0 0 0 0 0 0
0 0 0 0 0 0 0 0 0 0 0 0 0 0 1 1 0 0 0 0 0 0 0 0 0 0 0 0 0 0 0 0 0 0 0 0
1 1 0 1 0 0 0 0 0 0 0 0 0 0 0 0 0 0 0 0 0 0 1 1 0 1 0 0 0 0 0 0 0 0 0 0
0 0 0 0 0 0 0 1 0 1 0 1 0 0 0 0 0 0 0 0 0 0 0 0 0 0 0 0 0 0 0 1 1 1 1 1 0
0 0 0 0 0 0 0 0 0 0 0 0 0 0 0 0 0 0 0 0 0 0 0 0 0 0 0 0 0 0 1 1 0 0 0 0
1 1 1 0 0 0 1 1 0 0 0 0 1 1 0 0 0 1 0 0 0 0 0 0 0 0 0 0 0 0 1 1 0 0 1 0
0 0 0 1 1 0 1 0 0 0 1 1 0 0 0 1 1 0 0 0 0 1 1 0 1 0 1 1 1 1 1 0 1 1 1 1 1
0 1 1 1 1 1 0 1 1 1 1 1 0 0 0 0 0 0 0 0 0 0 0 0 0 0 0 0 0 0 0 0 0 0 0 0
0 1 0 0 0 0 0 0 0 0 0 0 0 0 0 1 0 0 0 0 0 0 0 0 0 0 0 0 0 0 0 0 0 0 0 0
0 0 0 0 0 0 0 0 0 0 1 0 0 0 0 0 0 0 0 0 0 0 0 0 0 1 1 1 1 1 1 0 0
0 0 0 0 0 0 0 0 0 1 1 1 1 1 0 0 0 0 0 0 0 0 0 0 0 0 0 0 0 0 0 0 0 0
0 0 1 1 0 0 0 0 1 1 0 0 0 0 1 1 1 0 0 0 1 1 0 0 0 1 0 0 0 0 0 0 1 0 0 0
0 0 0 0 0 0 1 0 0 0 0 1 1 0 1 0 0 0 0 1 1 0 0 0 1 1 1 0 0 1 1 0 1 0 1 1 1
1 1 0 1 1 1 1 1 0 1 1 1 1 1 1 0 1 1 1 1 1 0 0 0 0 0 0 0 0 0 0 0 0 0 0 0
0 0 0 0 0 0 0 0 1 0 0 0 0 0 0 1 1 0 0 0 0 0 0 0 0 0 1 0 0 0 0 0 0 0 0 0
0 0 1 1 0 0 0 0 0 0 0 0 0 0 0 0 1 0 0 0 0 0 0 1 1 0 0 0 0 0 0 0 0 0 0 0
1 1 1 1 1 1 0 0 0 0 1 1 0 0 0 0 0 1 1 1 1 0 0 0 0 0 0 0 0 0 0 1 1 0
0 0 0 0 0 0 0 0 0 0 0 1 0 0 0 0 0 0 0 1 0 0 0 0 0 0 0 1 0 0 0 0 0 1
0 0 0 0 0 1 1 0 0 0 0 0 0 0 1 0 0 0 0 0 0 0 0 1 1 0 0 0 1 1 0 0 0 0 0 0
1 0 0 0 0 0 0 0 0 0 1 1 0 0 0 1 0 0 0 0 1 1 0 0 0 0 0 0 0 0 0 0 0 0 0
0 1 1 0 0 1 1 0 0 0 0 0 0 0 0 0 0 0 0 1 1 0 0 0 1 0 0 0 0 0 1 1 0 0 0 0 0
0 0 0 0 1 1 0 0 0 0 0 1 0 0 0 0 0 0 0 1 0 0 0 0 0 1 0 0 0 0 1 0 0 0
0 0 0 0 0 1 0 0 0 0 0 0 0 0 0 1 0 0 0 1 0 0 0 0 0 0 0 0 0 1 0 0 0 0 0 0
1 0 0 0 0 1 0 0 0 0 0 0 1 0 0 0 0 0 0 1 0 0 0 0 0 1 0 0 0 0 0 1 0 0 0 0
0 0 0 0 0 0 1 1 0 0 0 0 0 0 0 0 1 1 0 0 0 0 0 0 0 0 1 1 0 0 0 0 0 0 0
0 1 0 0 0 1 1 1 0 1 0 1 1 0 0 0 0 0 0 0 0 0 1 0 0 0 0 0 1 1 0 1 1 0 0 0
0 0 0 0 0 0 0 0 0 1 0 0 0 0 0 1 1 1 1 0 0 0 0 0 0 0 0 0 0 1 0 0 0
0 1 0 1 1 1 0 1 0 0 1 0 1 1 0 1 1 0 0 0 0 0 1 0 0 1 1 1 1 0 0 1 0 0 1 1 1
1 1 1 1 0 1 1 1 0 0 0 0 1 1 1 0 0 0 0 0 1 1 0 1 1 1 0 0 0 0 0 0 0 0 1 0
1 0 0 0 0 0 1 1 1 0 1 1 0 0 1 0 0 0 0 0 0 1 0 1 0 0 0 0 0 1 1 1 1 1 0 0
1 0 0 0 0 0 1 0 1 0 0 0 0 0 1 1 0 0 0 0 0 1 0 0 0 0 0 1 1 0 1 1 0 0 0
0 0 0 0 0 0 0 0 0 0 0 0 0 0 0 0 0 0 0 0 0 0 0 0 0 0 0 0 1 1 1 0 0
0 0 0 1 0 0 0 0 0 0 0 0 0 0 0 0 1 1 1 0 1 0 1 0 0 0 1 0 1 0 1 0 1 0 1
0 1 0 0 1 1 1 0 0 0 0 0 0 0 0 0 1 0 1 0 1 0 0 0 0 0 0 0 0 0 0 0 0 0
0 0 1 0 1 0 0 0 0 0 0 0 0 0 0 0 1 1 1 1 0 0 0 0 0 0 0 0 0 0 0 0 0
0 0 0 1 1 1 1 1 1 1 0 0 0 0 0 0 0 0 0 0 1 1 1 0 0 0 0 0 0 1 1 1
0 0 0 0 0 0 0 0 1 1 0 0 0 0 0 0 0 0 1 1 0 0 0 0 0 0 1 1 0 1 0 0
0 0 0 0 0 0 0 1 0 1 1 0 0 0 0 1 1 0 0 1 1 0 0 0 0 0 0 1 1 0 0 1 1 0 0
0 0 1 0 0 0 1 0 1 0 0 0 0 0 1 0 1 0 0 0 1 0 0 0 1 0 0 1 0 0 1 0 0 0
0 0 1 0 0 0 1 0 0 0 0 0 0 0 1 0 0 0 1 0 1 0 0 0 1 0 0 0 0 0 0 0 0
0 1 0 0 0 0 1 0 0 0 0 1 0 0 0 0 0 0 0 0 0 0 0 1 0 0 0 0 0 0 0 0 1 0 0
0 0 0 0 0 0 0 0 0 0 1 0 0 1 0 1 0 0 0 0 0 0 0 0 0 0 0 1 1 1 1 0 0 1 1
1 1 1 0 1 0 0 1 1 1 1 0 0 0
```

The Arecibo message consisted of 1,679 zeros and ones.

The message consists of exactly 1,679 bits of information. The number was chosen because it is the product of 23 × 73 and no other pair of numbers. Experts hope that any ET receiving the message will know this and divide the bits into 23 columns of 73 bits each.

Each bit of information is a short on or off burst of radio waves. Using the binary number system, the pattern corresponds to a series of 0s and 1s. To

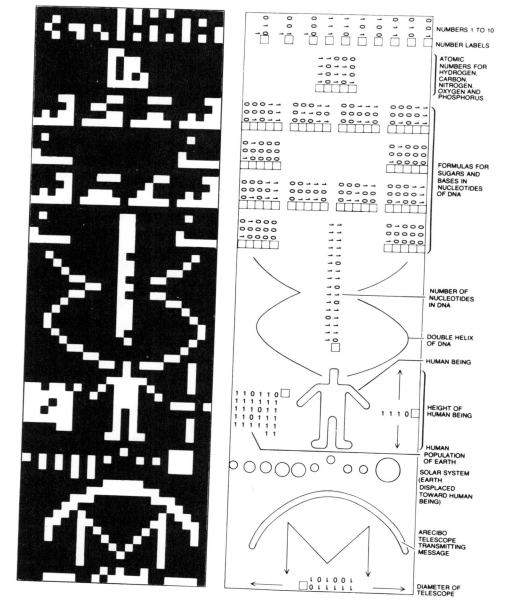

NUMBERS 1 TO 10

NUMBER LABELS

ATOMIC NUMBERS FOR HYDROGEN, CARBON, NITROGEN, OXYGEN AND PHOSPHORUS

FORMULAS FOR SUGARS AND BASES IN NUCLEOTIDES OF DNA

NUMBER OF NUCLEOTIDES IN DNA

DOUBLE HELIX OF DNA

HUMAN BEING

HEIGHT OF HUMAN BEING

HUMAN POPULATION OF EARTH

SOLAR SYSTEM (EARTH DISPLACED TOWARD HUMAN BEING)

ARECIBO TELESCOPE TRANSMITTING MESSAGE

DIAMETER OF TELESCOPE

If intelligent beings in space receive and understand the Arecibo message, they will find it includes all this information. Illustration by Ilil Arbel from *The Search for Extraterrestrial Intelligence* by Carl Sagan and Frank Drake. Copyright © 1975 by Scientific American, Inc. All rights reserved.

anyone who understands, or can figure out, the binary system, the message will show:

—the numbers from 1 to 10;

—the atomic numbers for several common elements;

—the formula for DNA;

—the human population on Earth;

—and pictures of the double helix of DNA, a human being, the solar system and the Arecibo telescope, that are visible if the ons and offs are made different colors.

Radio waves travel as fast as light waves. At that rate it should take 25,000 years for the message to reach its destination. Should some ET understand the communication and reply *immediately,* it will take another 25,000 years for the answer to reach Earth!

The latest idea for making contact with ETs is the brainchild of John D. G. Rather, a leading expert on lasers. He suggests that instead of using radio waves, we should be looking for and sending out beams of laser light.

Laser beams travel as fast and as far as radio waves. And they can carry the same kinds of signals and messages. More advanced civilizations would surely know about lasers. Lasers might even prove to be more efficient for communicating over long distances. Thus far, though, laser communication has not been tried.

Visiting ETs

Receiving a radio or laser message from an ET would be a remarkable event for humanity. But even more thrilling is the possibility of actually visiting an alien civilization. Why, then, aren't more scientists planning missions to planets on which life might exist?

Travel to another planet is extremely hazardous, difficult and expensive. It requires a gigantic amount of fuel and takes a very, very long time. Radio waves, as we have said, travel at the speed of light—186,000 miles per second. Even if we could supply enough energy to send a spacecraft at nearly that speed—which right now is completely impossible—because of speeding up and slowing down, it would probably take at least ten years to reach the nearest star, Alpha Centauri. (Alpha Centauri is only 4.3 light-years away from Earth.)

Thus far there is no evidence of planets or ETs anywhere near Alpha Centauri. While we might be lucky and find ETs 5 or 10 light-years distant, it is more likely that the nearest ET is on a planet that is 10,000 or 20,000 light-years away.

Two possible ways to manage such a super-long trip are being considered. One involves the use of huge spaceships on which many generations could live. The other depends upon putting people into a state of suspended animation that vastly extends their lifetimes.

Right now, there is no known way of moving at more than a fraction of the speed of light. Our fastest, most modern rockets would take several thousand years just to get to Alpha Centauri. Using the most perfect nuclear fusion engine that scientists can conjure up, it would still take an estimated 1.6 billion tons of fuel for every ton of payload.

A 100 percent efficient matter-antimatter engine, one that is still only in the dream stage, would need about 34 tons of fuel for every ton of payload. Thus, a trip to Alpha Centauri would use up more energy than the entire population of Earth has obtained from all the coal, oil and gas it has burnt, plus all the atoms it has split for nuclear energy, since history began! When compared with the small cost of sending a radio or laser signal, the cost of a manned voyage to the far reaches of our galaxy is almost impossible to imagine.

What about the possibility of ETs coming to visit us on Earth?

Right now we believe that nothing in the universe can travel faster than the speed of light. Thus, ETs would have to solve the same problems if they tried to reach us. Unless, of course, they have a way of moving faster than light that we don't know about.

Dr. Rather has a far-out dream about covering immense distances very quickly. He thinks that one day it will be possible to encode all the biological information necessary to create a living being and to send it on a laser beam anywhere in the universe. Based on the instructions, the creature could then be assembled at the new location, no matter how distant. If this ever becomes a reality, a trip to another civilization would be much more likely.

Some scientists, among them British astronomer Sir Martin Ryle, fear an alien invasion of our planet. ETs might be hostile, he says, coming here to enslave or kill all humans.

Others quarrel with his position. They claim that ETs advanced enough to reach Earth would probably not want or need anything we have here and would have no desire to conquer Earth. It also seems to make little sense for ETs to undertake so long and difficult a journey only to have to battle the inhabitants when they arrive.

But suppose the ETs are fleeing a catastrophe or severe overcrowding on their home planet. What then?

Experts don't believe that ETs would choose Earth as a place to settle. More likely they would prefer some uninhabited planet. Still, the idea of not trying to make contact merely in order to keep our existence and location secret is generally not accepted. The need to expand the boundaries of our knowledge is too strong to be governed by fear.

4

VISITORS FROM SPACE

**Visitors from Space: physical evidence on
Earth that extraterrestrials have been here.**

About 250 miles southeast of Lima, Peru, is the plain of Nazca. It is a barren, desertlike strip of land about 40 miles long and 5 miles wide. Carved into the dark soil of the plain are more than 13,000 lines, along with drawings of nearly 800 huge birds, fish, lizards, spiders and monkeys. The lines were etched into the ground by removing the surface rocks to expose the lighter soil beneath. Scientists guess that they were drawn about 2,000 years ago.

Many have wondered about these markings since they were first discovered in 1927. Neither the modern descendants of the Incas nor scholars studying the area have been able to determine their purpose. Some thought they were roads. But most roads go somewhere; these go nowhere.

One popular idea is that the lines on the Nazca plain were made by ETs who used the plain as a spaceport. According to this theory, an alien spaceship landed there and found it a good landing site. The astronauts then made the lines in the surface to guide them for future landings.

Some believe that the lines on the Nazca plain show that it was used as a spaceport by visitors from space.

In several places the lines do look like the runways of a modern airport. And because they are several miles long, the pattern can easily be seen from space.

That is one possible explanation for the lines. But what about the animal drawings? One suggestion is that the ETs made several landings at the space-

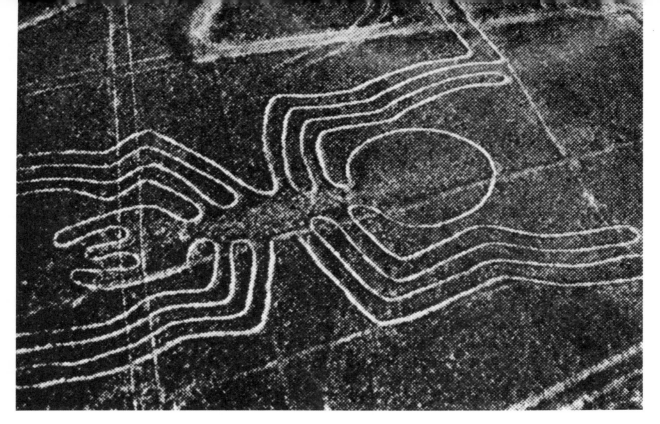

The giant animal drawings on the plain of Nazca could have been drawn by the natives to attract ETs.

port and then stopped coming. To attract them back, the natives drew pictures of the giant animals on the Nazca plain.

Then there is the question of how the drawings of the figures were made. They are almost impossible to visualize from ground level; the entire size and shape can be seen only from the air. But people in Peru did not have airborne vehicles 2,000 years ago.

Could both the lines and the animals have been inscribed by visitors from space?

• • •

The great pyramids of Egypt are stunning achievements of design and construction. They date back nearly 5,000 years. But how could they have been built? From what is known of history, there were too few workers in the entire Middle East for this monumental task. And given the primitive tools and lack of knowledge about building at the time, it would have taken thousands of workers several hundreds of years to finish each pyramid!

History also tells us that there was not enough food growing in the desert to feed the workers. Nor was there housing for them to live in. There would not have been tools to cut, move and raise the 12-ton blocks of stone nor engineers to plan a structure that even today would require dozens of blueprints and the most advanced tools and equipment.

How, then, did the ancient Egyptians suddenly become able to assemble the manpower and develop the planning and building skills that went into the pyramids? Did they have help from outside the boundaries of Earth?

• • •

The Dogons are a tribal group living in what is now the Republic of Mali in West Africa. Even today they have very little scientific information and few research tools. Yet, some of their most ancient legends show an amazing knowledge of astronomy.

The ancient Dogon sacred writings and tribal myths contain facts that scientists have gleaned only in the last hundred years or so using the most modern telescopes and other advanced instruments. Among these facts is the following information:

• Sirius, the Dog Star, has a companion star.
• Sirius and its companion circle each other every fifty years.
• The companion star is very small and is made of the heaviest metal in the universe.
• Jupiter has four moons.
• Saturn has a ring.
• The planets move in elliptical orbits.

These same Dogon texts describe the arrival on Earth of a creature called a *Nommo*. He is described as a being who can live both on land and in the water; a "cross between a man and a dolphin." The *Nommo*, according to the Dogons, landed on Earth in an "ark" that raised a "whirlwind" of dust.

How did the Dogons acquire their knowledge? Was the *Nommo* an astronaut from a different planet? Was the ark his spaceship? Was the whirlwind the rocket exhaust? And was the *Nommo* the individual who taught the Dogons about astronomy?

• • •

Erich von Däniken, a self-taught expert in ETs, has devoted his life to searching the world for evidence of visits by creatures from outer space. In his book *The Gold of the Gods*, he tells how in 1965, explorer Juan Moricz was on an expedition among the Indian tribes of Ecuador in South America. Moricz wanted to learn more about their folklore and customs. One day, deep in the tropical jungle, he came upon a great doorway cut into some rock. Passing through, Moricz found himself slipping, sliding and climbing down to a depth of nearly 800 feet.

At the bottom, Moricz entered an amazing underworld of caves and tunnels. Some of the tunnels were narrow; some wide. There were walls, both rough and smooth, covered with a shiny glaze. Certain surfaces seemed to have been carved out by rapidly flowing water in the distant past; others appeared to have been blasted open by powerful explosions.

Moricz was particularly struck by the fact that all the tunnels met at right angles. He guessed that the system of tunnels extended for hundreds and hundreds of miles, perhaps beneath the entire continent of South America.

Down one hall he came upon a mammoth room the size of an airplane hangar for a jumbo jet. In the center was a massive table with seven chairs, all made of mysterious material that was neither wood, metal, stone nor plastic. Behind the chairs was a whole collection of animal statues—elephants, lions, crocodiles, bears, monkeys and wolves, with snails and crabs scattered between them. All were made of solid gold!

In the other tunnels and rooms were many more carvings—of gold, rare metals and stone. One particularly interesting stone amulet showed a human figure standing on a globe that appears to be marked off with latitude and longitude lines. The right hand held a symbol of the moon, the left a sign of the sun. Another stone bore a carving of a dinosaur on its surface. Also in this great hall was a library of over 2,000 metal pages that looked like large sheets of paper. Each sheet was covered with strange writing that neither Moricz nor anyone else could understand.

Who dug the tunnels? And why?

Erich von Däniken suggested this possible explanation: Very long ago there was a cosmic battle between creatures who resembled humans and another, different race of beings. The humanoids lost and fled to planet Earth. Before landing on Earth, though, they first set up powerful radio transmitters on a planet that was in orbit between Mars and Jupiter. Their hope was to fool the victors into thinking that they had landed there.

When they arrived on Earth, they dug these tunnels as a hiding place. At the same time, the victors, thinking they were on the other planet, exploded it into tiny bits. The pieces became the asteroids that are now in orbit in a belt between Mars and Jupiter.

Afraid that they might all be killed, the humanoid losers wrote down the story of their race on the long-lasting metal sheets inside the tunnels. When they felt safe they came up out of their hiding places. They began to create a new race in their image. Relying on their advanced knowledge in biology, they began breeding the monkeys of South America to start the evolutionary process that led, over millions of years, to the human race.

• • •

On Easter Sunday 1722, the Dutch explorer Jacob Roggeveen discovered a tiny dot of an island in the South Pacific, about 2,300 miles west of Chile. He named it Easter Island.

The most striking feature of Easter Island remains the hundreds of huge stone statues that Roggeveen found there, dating back to A.D. 400. All show heads only, which range in size from 33 to 66 feet. The largest ones weigh as much as 50 tons. They are carved from the very hard volcanic rock on which the island was formed.

Many observers find it hard to believe that these statues were carved by the Easter Island natives. The barren land there produces little food and cannot support more than 2,000 inhabitants—too few to have produced all the statues that have been found, even if they worked day and night.

Did visitors from space make the huge stone heads on Easter Island?

The only tools found at the carving sites were small stone picks. The picks seem wholly unfit for the job of carving the giant statues out of the rock.

There are also no signs of trees on the island, then or now. Without rollers made of tree trunks, the Indians could not have moved the massive carvings from the interior mountains where they were carved to the coast where they are now. And no one can figure out how the natives were able to raise them to an upright position.

Who carved, transported and erected the Easter Island statues?

The great stone carvings of Easter Island have been explained as everything from part of a long-lost continent to the work of ancient ETs.

In checking out the Easter Island heads, Erich von Däniken found that the natives call their island Land of the Bird Men. Ancient legends tell how men with wings landed here bringing fire to the island. Von Däniken believes that this myth really describes ETs who arrived by spaceship and became stranded on this tiny bit of land in the middle of the Pacific Ocean. While awaiting rescue they used their advanced tools to carve these statues to resemble themselves. The proof that von Däniken offers is the fact that none of the Easter Island natives look like the statues, which show faces with long, straight noses, sunken eyes, tight lips and low foreheads.

Von Däniken believes that in time the ETs left. And the Easter Island people tried to create similar statues with their much more primitive tools. Unable to succeed, they flung down their stone picks—instruments that can still be found around the quarries.

• • •

Near the Yucatán Peninsula of Mexico, in the ancient Mayan city of Palenque, there is a 70-foot-high pyramid known as the Temple of the Inscriptions. Buried 65 feet beneath the pyramid is believed to be the tomb of the god Kulkulkán. When scientists first discovered the tomb in 1949, they were amazed by the carved lid.

The ancient Mayan Temple of the Inscriptions is found near the Yucatan Peninsula of Mexico.

The lid shows Kulkulkán seated in what appears to be a spaceship, leaning forward like someone riding a motorcycle. The craft comes to a point in front, where there is a magnetic device to repel particles that might damage the craft in flight. Flames can be seen shooting out the back. The ancient "astronaut" is wearing a space suit, with tight bands at the neck, wrists and ankles. On his face is an oxygen mask. With his hands he is working the controls. His feet are operating the foot pedals.

Yet, the tomb and pyramid were built around A.D. 700—long before anyone in Mexico or elsewhere knew about rockets or spaceships!

Could the image show an ancient astronaut from an advanced civilization who landed on Earth in those primitive times?

Does this tomb carving, which dates back to the 8th century, show Kulkulkán riding a space-ship?

• • •

Early on the morning of June 30, 1908, a huge fireball was seen flashing across the sky of Siberia. It smashed down to Earth in the remote Tunguska region with a blinding flash of light and an earth-shattering explosion. Afterward, observers described a tall "pillar of fire" arising from the point of impact.

The force of the explosion was so strong that people 38 miles away felt the searing heat on their skin. The impact shattered windows of houses 50 miles away. A passing train, 440 miles distant, was almost knocked off its tracks. And people throughout Europe and Asia trembled because of the shock waves.

At first scientists believed the loud disturbance was caused by a meteorite falling to Earth. But members of the first expedition to reach the blast site, in 1927, doubted that this was so. The crash of a meteorite would have dug out a big, deep crater. Instead, the investigators found that the impact had just flattened nearly 2,000 square miles of the forest and left it completely clean of trees.

The fireball that smashed down in Siberia in 1908 flattened nearly 2,000 square miles of forest.

A meteorite landing with such an impact had to contain tons of metal and stone; but no traces of either material were found. Even when they drilled far beneath the surface, scientists discovered no remnants of a meteor. Also, the high levels of radioactivity measured at the site would not have been caused by a meteor.

Was the mysterious "fireball" a spacecraft from another world that crashed when it landed on Earth?

• • •

Each of these reports is disputed by experts on both sides of the issue. On one side are those who say that the unexplained events prove that ETs have landed on Earth. The various objects, traces or monumental achievements of labor are positive evidence of their visits. Against this view are those who say that each account can be understood in much more ordinary ways. Several scientists have indeed come up with a number of easier-to-believe explanations of the phenomena described above.

The Plain of Nazca
There are a few reasons for doubting that the Nazca plain was ever a space-port for ETs. Rocket ships land and take off straight up and down; unlike airplanes, they don't need long runways. And rockets would find it very difficult to land or take off from the soft, sandy soil of Nazca.

Dr. Paul Kosok, one of the first scientists to study the plain of Nazca, thinks that the lines are actually an ancient astronomical calendar. According to his calculations, several of the lines point to the positions of the sun, moon and certain bright stars on the important days that mark each of the four seasons.

About a dozen lines, Kosok found, pass through the animal figures. The figures may be there, he thinks, just to identify the particular lines. Or else

Some of the drawings in Nazca show strange, fanciful creatures. (left)

Dr. Paul Kosok believes that the animal figures on the Nazca plain are drawings of constellations. (right)

the animals may be constellations of stars as seen from the Nazca region.

Then there is the matter of the difficulty of drawing the huge animal figures without seeing them from above. It is possible, says the International Explorers Society, that the Incas knew how to make man-carrying, lighter-than-air smoke balloons. The artist could then view his work from over the

plain and make any necessary corrections. Samples of tightly woven fabric and rope that could be used in making the balloons survive. And even the clay pots for holding the fire have been found. In fact, in 1975, some IES members made a balloon of natural materials and flew over the plain for a perfect view of the figures!

The Egyptian Pyramids

The idea that the pyramids in Egypt were built by visitors from outer space is a long-held theory. It is often used to explain how the Egyptians were suddenly, without any preparation, able to erect these amazing monuments.

Careful research, though, shows that the pyramids did not instantly appear in full perfection: The Egyptians went through a slow process of development, with many errors.

The earliest royal tombs, starting around 3100 B.C., were little more than boxes of mud and brick resting on the ground. Over the following centuries this type of structure grew bigger and more elaborate, climaxing in the Step Pyramid of Zoser built around 2700 B.C.

Some of the early Egyptian pyramids were nothing more than huge piles of mud and stone.

The Step Pyramid of Zoser, built in 2700 BC.

The pyramid at Medum was being built in the familiar pyramid shape— until it collapsed!

The builders changed the angle of the Dashur pyramid to prevent its collapse.

The first tomb in the familiar pyramid shape was erected at Medum in 2630 B.C.—but it collapsed. Soon after, the so-called Bent Pyramid of Dashur was built. The sharp change in angle of slope is thought to be a correction made after construction began. Modern engineers calculate that the entire structure would have collapsed without the change. Based on what they learned from these earlier pyramids, the Egyptians then built the three renowned pyramids at Giza without error. Even then it took several centuries to complete them.

The Dogon Myths

The Dogons have long worshipped Sirius, the Dog Star. It is the brightest star in the sky and its appearance every year is a signal that the flood season is about to begin. For this reason, Sirius has always played an especially important part in the Dogons' myths.

But how did the amazingly accurate astronomical information become part of their ancient Dogon legends? Researchers in the history of science have no reason to believe that travelers from outer space landed among the Dogons and gave them this knowledge. They have a different explanation.

During the 1920s there was a great deal of public interest in Sirius B, the companion star to Sirius. Many now think that a European trader or missionary told the Dogons about Sirius B—including its fifty-year orbit and its great weight. Since many of the Europeans living in Africa were amateur astronomers, it is also likely that they let the Dogons look through their telescopes. Through even a weak telescope, the Dogons would have been able to see the moons of Jupiter (there are fourteen, not four) and the rings of Saturn. Over the years, the tribal members probably incorporated this new information into their old legends. And so by now they are convinced that they knew about Sirius and the other stars and planets hundreds of years ago.

The Tunnels of Ecuador

The legend of the fabulous tunnels can be traced back to tales written in the 1930s by an Ecuadorian soldier, Captain Jaramillo. It was these tales that led Moricz to start looking for the tunnels.

But the tunnels Moricz saw were nowhere near as splendid as those von Däniken described. They were very ordinary tunnels and caves that had been carved into the ground and rock by flowing underwater streams. Moricz later insisted, "If he [von Däniken] claims to have seen the library and the other things himself, then that's a lie."

Easter Island

In 1955, the Norwegian explorer and anthropologist Thor Heyerdahl led an exploratory expedition to Easter Island. He found that the volcanic rock of the statues was quite soft and could be chipped away with the harder stone picks the carvers used. And he discovered that the stone is even softer when wet.

At Heyerdahl's request, a group of six islanders showed the scientist how they could remove the rough outline of the figure from the solid rock in just three days. At that rate it would take two teams of six men each about one year to carve a single medium-sized statue. And they also demonstrated how they were able to transport and erect the stone figures.

It was hard work. And it did take a long time. But it surely was within the abilities of the islanders, without help from ETs.

The Palenque "Astronaut"

Not all people see the same thing when looking at the same object. When von Däniken looks at the tomb lid, he sees someone seated in a spaceship. But many anthropologists don't see it this way at all.

The anthropologists point out that the so-called astronaut is seated on, rather than in, the "rocket." He is seated on the Mayan Earth monster, a symbol that he was king. The rocket itself, experts say, is a combination of a cross and a two-headed serpent.

The "magnetic device" at the tip of the rocket is a quetzal, a bird sacred to the Mayas. The man is not wearing a space suit, but a breech cloth, with anklets, bracelets, necklace and headpiece—a typical Mayan outfit. Since his toes and fingers are visible, we know he is wearing neither shoes nor gloves.

The "controls" in his hands are parts of the drawings of the Mayan sun god. The "pedal" beneath his feet is a seashell, the representation of death.

And the "flames" in the rear are the roots of the sacred corn plant.

To clinch their argument, the anthropologists have brought forth historical records proving that the lid was on the tomb of the Mayan king Pacal, who died in A.D. 693.

The Explosion at Tunguska

Soon after the first atom bomb was exploded in 1945, some people recalled the 1908 incident at Tunguska. They compared the two, and said that the Tunguska occurrence was like an atom bomb explosion—tremendous force, blinding light, powerful shock waves—even the mushroom cloud ("pillar of fire"). A Russian engineer, Alexander Kazantsev, theorized that an ET spaceship, powered by nuclear energy, had tried to land on Earth. But it ran into technical difficulties and the nuclear engine exploded, just like an atom bomb.

A Russian geologist and chemist, Kirill P. Florensky, led expeditions to the Tunguska site in 1958, 1961 and 1962. After careful investigation, Florensky

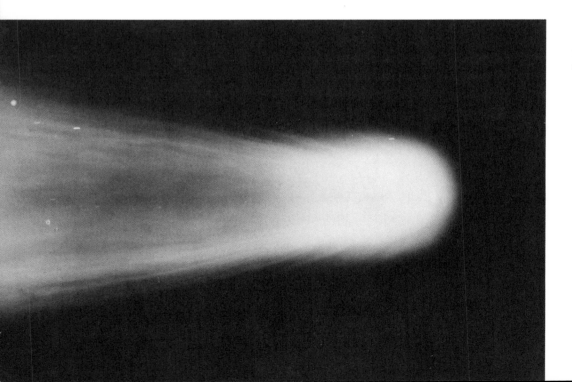

It is now believed that the fireball that crashed to Earth in Siberia was a comet.

decided that a very large comet, not ETs, struck Earth and exploded on that fateful morning.

Astronomers call comets "dirty snowballs." They contain a lot of dust held together by ice and other frozen gases. As comets enter the Earth's atmosphere, the ice immediately changes to gas. As the gas bursts out, it causes a powerful explosion.

At the same time, the friction of passing through the atmosphere at an estimated 2 miles per second causes the comet to glow brightly. By the time it strikes the Earth, though, there is not enough matter to create a crater. As for the high level of radioactivity reported, Florensky found no hint of unusual readings.

Summary

This book has explored the many ways scientists have searched for life in outer space. In the case of UFOs, they have found ordinary, natural explanations for all but a few of the reported sightings. Still, they hesitate to state positively that there are no UFOs. The unsolved cases mean that there is some possibility that UFOs really do exist.

Scientists, however, take the search for ETs much more seriously. No one has yet succeeded in making contact with alien beings after some thirty years of trying. Nevertheless, many are convinced that there are other civilizations in outer space and that in time we will be able to communicate with their members.

Almost everyone agrees that the evidence of visitors from outer space is rather weak. Still, few want to rule out completely the possibility of such an event. Perhaps there were landings that we don't know about. Or maybe there are even alien creatures on Earth right now that we cannot see!

UFOs, ETs and visitors from space are subjects of great wonder—and of many unresolved questions. That is why they are so endlessly fascinating!

Glossary

Alien Someone from a different land—or a different planet.

Apollo 11 Launched July 16, 1969, this was the first space shot to land humans on the moon, on July 20th. The mission returned to Earth on July 24, 1969.

Astronaut A highly trained man or woman who flies in the space shuttle and other spacecraft launched from Earth.

Ball lightning Lightning that takes the shape of a ball instead of a long streak. The ball can be several feet across. Ball lightning is seen either falling from a cloud or rolling along the ground.

ET Abbreviation of extraterrestrial, a creature that may or may not resemble a human, coming not from Earth, but from elsewhere in the universe.

Flying saucer Another name for UFO. *See also UFO.*

Hertz A unit of frequency named after the German physicist Heinrich

Hertz (1857–1894). A hertz (abbreviated Hz) equals one cycle per second.

IFO   Abbreviation of *i*dentified *f*lying *o*bject. An object, sighted in space or on the ground, that is first believed to be a UFO, but is later identified. *See also UFO.*

Light-year   The distance that light, traveling at 186,000 miles per second, will cover in one year. A light-year is about 6 trillion miles. It is used to describe the immense distances between stars and galaxies.

Project Blue Book   The section within the U.S. Air Force that was devoted to the investigation of all reported UFO sightings. Project Blue Book was ended in 1969.

Pulsar   A huge star that has collapsed and is emitting pulses of radio waves.

Radio telescope   A telescope built to collect natural radio signals from distant points in space. It usually looks like a giant television antenna dish.

SETI   Abbreviation of *s*earch for *e*xtra*t*errestrial *i*ntelligence, the current search for some means of establishing communication with other intelligent beings in the universe.

UFO   Abbreviation of *u*nidentified *f*lying *o*bject, an object, usually sighted by one person or a small number of people, that appears to be a spaceship from an alien civilization.

Index